The Vikings

A thousand years ago, pagans from the North spread fear and terror all over of Europe. For more than two hundred years they sailed on their *Viking expeditions* from the coasts of Scandinavia - as pirates, as merchants, and as aggressors.

Before archaeological finds had come to light, our knowledge about the Viking Age was based on the *sagas* - these stories from the history of an earlier past were related and written down during the Middle Ages. But the archaeological evidence, once it had been found, not only adds to these literary sources - it also gives a different and more varied picture of this ancient history. Excavations not only supplement our knowledge of history - as a result of them, our understanding of history is forever changing.

But one aspect remains unchanged: our idea of the Viking Age as a period when people from the region we now know as Scandinavia set out far beyond their own lands, and left their mark on the countries they came to. And as a result, their home-lands also changed - the first to voyage out, towards the end of the eighth century, set out from a pagan society led by local chieftains; by the end of the Viking Age, during the eleventh century, the Scan-dinavian countries had become realms where power lay in the hands of kings and the Church.

Cemetery, Lindholm Høye, Denmark.

A Burial

Burials constitute our most important archaeological source for the history of the Viking Age. The Norse burial rites had been laid down by *Odin,* supreme among the gods. He had decreed that all the dead must be burned, and that all their property must accompany them on the funereal pyre, for they must have all their possessions with them when they come to Valhall. The ashes must either be scattered over the sea or buried on land. Burial mounds must be raised to commemorate chieftains and other great men.

A unique report dealing with the funeral of a Viking merchant chieftain, comes from Ibn Fadlan, an Arab delegate on the shores of the Volga. The following is the gist of his story:

For ten days, while preparations for the funeral are going on, the deceased lies covered in a grave. These preparations were always led by an old woman. One of his bondswomen is to accompany the dead chieftain, and she is guarded all day and all night. She drinks every day. Now the ship is hauled up on land and set on logs, and the funeral can start. The dead chieftain, clad in his finest garb, is taken on board the ship. He is given fruit and plants, bread, meat and onions. All his weapons are laid by his side. A dog, cut in half, is put on board, together with two horses, who are stabbed to death with swords. Two cows, a hen and a cock complete the retinue. Six men have intercourse with the bondswoman in the tent where the dead chieftain lies, and afterwards, she is laid at the side of her dead lord. The men hold her while the old woman responsible for the funereal rites kills her by stabbing her between the ribs with a dagger, which goes right through her chest.

Now the chieftain's closest relative sets fire to the ship; afterwards all the others present throw burning brands on to the ship.

Left: In the course of the Viking Age, cremation was replaced by inhumation burial. Viking grave, Langeland, Denmark.

Right: Burial mound at Slinde in Sogn, Norway, after Thomas Fearnley's painting from 1839.

The Oseberg Find

In the summer of 1903 the farmer at *Oseberg* in the Norwegian county of Vestfold started to dig in a burial mound which lay on his land. It was 44 m in diameter and 2.5 m high. What he found there was of

such great interest that he contacted Professor Gabriel Gustafson (*above*) in Oslo. When Gustafson came to Oseberg two days later, it was immediately obvious to him that this find was sensational. No other find has ever equalled it in luxury or significance.

The mound housed a ship laden with a cart, four sledges, horsegear, textiles, tools and equipment for agriculture and needlework, a tent, beds, as well as much else. Fortunately it had been buried in clayey ground, which meant that wooden and leather objects, as well as textiles, were unusually well preserved. The skeletal remains show that this mound had been raised over two women - a young woman and an older one. The burial chamber in the aftership has enabled us to date the burial with great precision. An analysis of the annual rings on timber from the chamber has yielded the date AD 834 as the year of burial.

A Heavily Laden Ship

The carved decorations, as well as the low freeboard, indicate that the Oseberg Ship must have been a stately craft, built for *coastal sailing*. The clinker-built oaken ship could be rowed as well as sailed. She is 22 m long and 5 m in the beam amidships.

Viking ships were built as *shells*. Clinker-built hulls are self-supporting, but in order that the vessel should be able to withstand pressure from the sea and the strains of rowing and sailing, ribs were added inside the shell. It had taken several centuries, and the experience of many generations, before this method of boat-building was perfected. Originally such ships had been rowed only, with up to fifteen pairs of oars. Sails made their appearance once the hull - and especially the keel - was sturdy enough, while nevertheless retaining its elasticity. And that was the beginning of the Viking Age.

Top: A copy of the bed, internal length 1.7 m. It can be taken apart for purposes of transport.

Below right: Household equipment. The elaborate handle-attachment on the bucket is English or Irish.

The Sledges

The Oseberg burial held no fewer than four sledges, three of them luxuriantly ornamented. The man who made them was a worthy representative of his traditional craft. For the runners of two of the sledges, he joined two pieces of wood with a natural curvature, so that both ends curve upwards. The sledges themselves are made of beech-wood, but the lowest part of the runners, the wearing surface, is of oak.

The sledges were not used simply for tobogganing downhill. There is a sledge-pole for two horses, and traces of wear show that this is how the sledges were used. Winter and snow were no hindrance for transport - in fact they made communication easier in many places. With a sledge and horses one can cross land and water, rivers and bogs.

Oseberg tapestry, reconstructed from the fragment at the right.

The Oseberg Cart

Apart from the ship itself, the *cart* is the largest object from the Oseberg find. Unlike the rest of the grave furniture, it was never used. As both axle-trees and shafts were firmly fixed, the cart could only have been used on a straight stretch of land, being unable to turn a curve. Wheeled transport is a later phenomenon in the North.

The function of this cart must have been ceremonial - it seems most likely that it should have been used in cultic processions. One of the tapestries (*above*) shows such a procession, with several carts taking part. The fertility cult of the Germanic peoples included a rite according to which the divinity, placed in a cart and covered, was driven across the fields in order to ensure a good harvest. The carts on the tapestry are covered, but

the symbols surrounding them would seem to show that one of the divinities in question must be *Frøya*, the goddess of love and fertility. Moreover, the principal motif at the rear of the cart is her ritual animal, the cat. The watchman of the gods, *Heimdall*, may also be represented on the cart, possibly by one of the male heads, where the artist has stressed the teeth (page 6). Heimdall, who was also a god, had teeth of gold.

The Oseberg burial is by far the most luxuriant of all the Viking Age burials known to us, and as such it has, ever since it was found, been associated with a queen and her bondswoman. But the strong cultic aspects may perhaps be taken to mean that the woman buried here was more than a queen, that she may have been Frøya's incarnation, her representative on earth.

The figure shown in the cart on this memorial stone from Gotland, Sweden, may perhaps represent Frøya.

19

The Sea and the Coast

Without the sea and the coast, there could hardly have been any Viking Age. The coasts of Scandinavia are indented by fjords and inlets, often divided from the ocean

by an archipelago of skerries. It was to this coast that the first people came after the Ice Age - here both sea and land could provide them with food. And in the following periods, too, most settlements were found here.

For those voyaging along the west coast of the Scandinavian peninsula, the coast was the *route to the north*. They called this coast *norveg*, the way to the north, and the land connected by this sea route was to become Noreg or Norge, the modern names for Norway in the two official Norwegian languages. And when the Vikings set out, as warriors and as princes, as emigrants and as merchants, the sea was their highway.

"The Island Trænen in Nordland". Painted by K. Baade, 1838.

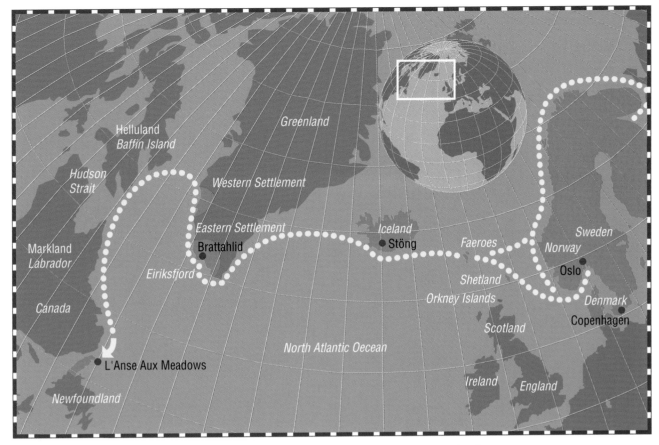

Helluland
Baffin Island

Greenland

Hudson
Strait

Western Settlement

Eastern Settlement

Iceland

Brattahlid ● ● Stöng

Faeroes

Sweden

Norway

Markland
Lábrador

Eiriksfjord

Oslo ●

Shetland

Denmark

Canada

Orkney Islands

● Copenhagen

Scotland

North Atlantic Oecean

L'Anse Aux Meadows

Ireland

England

Newfoundland

Iceland

The history of *Iceland, the Faeroes and Greenland* begins with the Viking Age. It was during this period that pioneers from the North emigrated, and established new settlements in the west, beyond the sea. The families who sailed westwards were farmers who left fjords and settlements which had become overpopulated; others emigrated in order to avoid living under the rule of Harald Fairhair, who ascended the throne in the 870s, as the first King of Norway. In Iceland, all free men could attend the annual *Thing,* and thereby take part in the government of the country. At the Thing they discussed politics, passed laws, and settled legal disputes.

The lands to which the emigrants came were almost completely uninhabited, and the Vikings must have been delighted when they found good pastures for their *livestock,* and a wealth of fish and fowl, seal and whale.

These islands lay far from the trade routes followed by merchants. Trade with the outside world was confined to essentials, for certain raw materials had to be obtained from elsewhere. The Icelanders could offer falcons and woollen materials, and in return they imported ships, corn, iron and soapstone. Once Greenland had been settled, in around 985, the produce of that country was also sold to the outside world.

Reconstruction of Viking Age houses, on the land of the farm Stöng in Iceland.

"Saga Siglar", Ragnar Thorseth's replica of a Viking ship found at Skuldelev in Denmark.

Greenland

The Saga of the Greenlanders tells us that this land was first settled by *Eirik the Red*, who organised an expedition of settlers from Iceland. His reason for settling in a new land was that he had been outlawed, and therefore he sailed out in order to find *"the land that Gunnbjørn sighted the time he was storm-driven west across the ocean"*. Eirik called the country he had found Greenland, *"for he argued that men would be drawn to go there if the land had an attractive name"*.

Eirik's ruse must have worked. His expedition consisted of as many as *25 ships*, and probably *something like five-hundred people -*

whole families, adults and children, with horses, sheep and cattle, with provisions and equipment. But eleven of the ships never reached Greenland - some had to turn back, others were wrecked.

Most of Greenland was covered by inland ice, as it is today. But Eirik led the settlers to the fjords on the west coast. Here they found good pasture, and here they

cleared land for their farms. Eirik had chosen the best of the fjords for himself, and there he built his chieftain's farm, Brattahlid, where he lived together with Thjodhild, his wife. It was here that *Leif Eiriksson* grew up.

"Saga Siglar" in a Greenland fjord.

Left: The Saga of the Greenlanders also includes an account of Leif Eiriksson's discovery of Vinland. The saga, which dates from around AD 1200, is preserved in this vellum manuscript from the end of the fourteenth century.

Right: The ruins of the church at Brattahlid, Eirik the Red's farm.

Vinland

Leif Eiriksson's youth was spent among bold sea-farers and farmers. One of these was *Bjarne Herjolfsson*, who had been driven off his route on his way home from Iceland, and he had then sighted land on the other side of the ocean. "There

was now much talk about voyages of discovery" says the saga. Leif bought Bjarne's ship, and found a crew. "There were thirty-five all told."

Leif and his crew prepared their ship, and sailed out to sea. They lighted on that land first which Bjarne had lighted on last. There was no grass

there, and Leif called the land *Helluland*, Flatstone Land. They sailed out to sea, and the next land they came to was covered with forest, and therefore Leif called this land *Markland*, Wood Land. After two more days at sea they came to a land where "there was dew on the grass, whereupon it happened to them that they set their

hands to the dew, then carried it to their mouths, and thought they had never known anything so sweet as that was." Leif called this land *Vinland.*

They built houses and spent the winter here. "There was no lack of salmon there in river or lake, and salmon bigger than they had ever seen before. The

26

nature of the land was so choice, it seemed to them that none of the cattle would require fodder for the winter. No frost came during the winter, and the grass was hardly withered."

"Leif Eiriksson sights America." Painted by Chr.Krohg, 1893.

Emigration to America

When summer came, Leif Eiriksson returned to Greenland. Both men and women were intrigued by the news of the new land, and they wished to try their luck there. Three different groups made for *Leifsbudir*, Leif's houses - but they returned to Greenland after a year or two. According to the saga, two of the groups were attacked by natives, while there was enmity and unrest in the third, resulting in conflict and murder. None found their fortune in Vinland.

L'Anse aux Meadows

Since the eighteenth century, scholars and others had been speculating about where one might find the Norse settlement in America. Numerous locations, from Florida in the south to Hudson Bay in the north, had been suggested. But the Norwegian author and discoverer *Helge Ingstad* was not satisfied with any of these theories, and in 1960 he went to Newfoundland together with his daughter *Benedicte*. They put the same question to all the people they met: Do you know of any traces or ruins of old houses hereabouts?

At L'Anse aux Meadows, by a bay where a brook runs out into the sea, they found the house-sites they had been searching for, surrounded by pasture land.

During the next eight summers Ingstad organised archaeological expeditions with scholars from five different countries. *Anne Stine Ingstad* was in charge of the archaeological work, and the excavations yielded eight house-sites, all of Norse type.

The objects found included two which confirm the Norse origin of the settlement: a ring-headed pin of bronze, and a soapstone spindle whorl. The saga tells us that women took part in the Vinland expeditions - the spindle whorl confirms this.

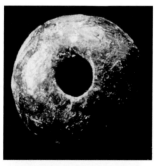

Combat and Religion

Åsgaard was the home of all the gods. *Odin* held all the others in his sway, for he was the eldest of them all. His supreme power and qualities covered many spheres - but he was first and foremost the god of war. The helmet he wore in battle was of the purest gold, and his spear never failed. His steed was the fastest of all horses, it had eight legs.

Thor, Odin's son, was also a warrior god. The strongest of them all, he was the protector of gods and men, defending them against giants and other horrors. His chief weapon was the hammer. The mountains shook and quivered when he drove across the skies, and fire flashed around him. He was the principal defender of the state of the world, and his tremendous strength enabled him to overcome the evil powers of the dark, intent upon upheaval and destruction. Wisdom and cunning were hardly his strongest points, but he was an expert with his hammer, *Mjølner.* Mjølner always found its mark, and then returned to its owner.

In a number of Germanic languages, *Wednesday* and *Thursday* bear the names of these two gods, Odin (or Wodan) and Thor.

Top: Thor, the ruler of the thunder, also caused rain to fall, and thus the fertility of the fields was also his domain.
"Thor Fighting the Giants", painted by Mårten Eskil Winge in 1872.

Left: Thor was extremely popular during the Viking Age, as finds of amulets and Thor's hammers of cast silver, wrought iron or carved amber show. Finds from Iceland and Sweden.

Right: Odin was the wisest of all the gods, but he had only one eye. The other he had given in exchange for a drink from the fountain of wisdom. This wooden sculpture was found in medieval Oslo.

Valhall

All those who fell in battle became Odin's foster sons. They came to *Valhall*, where Odin had a feast prepared for them every day. Nowhere was a hall greater than Valhall to be found - there were 640 doors there, each of them so wide that 960 warriors could pass through, shoulder by shoulder.

Every morning the warriors donned their armour, took up their arms, and went out into battle. But those who were killed, rose up again. And in the evening, they were all friends and shared the feast in Valhall.

Odin sent his female retainers, the *valkyries*, out into battles among mortal men, so that they might choose the warriors who were to die - and come to Valhall. There they were received by the valkyries, who offered them ale, and served at the feasts.

The fearless Vikings' religion stood them in good stead in their armed combats.

Right: The word valkyrie means "she who chooses the dead". The valkyries rode all over the world, through the air and over the ocean. Painting by P.N.Arbo, 1869.

Top: Several of the carved stones from Gotland have scenes illustrating life after death. This one is from Tjängvide. The building in the background may symbolise Valhall. The bearded horseman is most likely to be Odin; in any case, the horse is Sleipnir, his steed. The woman carrying a drinking horn may be a valkyrie - or perhaps she is Frøya? The braid with a knot may symbolise eternal and indivisible love - this was the essence of Viking Age women's petitions to Frøya.

Left: The motif on this silver dress ornament from Öland in Sweden also occurs on the stone from Tjängvide.

Arms and Amour

A thousand years of tradition went into the art of the Viking Age armorer when he fashioned axes, swords, spears and arrows of wrought iron. The craft of the smith was highly developed, and many of the weapons that have come down to us may well be said to be works of art. Wrought iron axes, knives and swords had cutting edges of tempered steel, a sophisticated refinement essential for warriors determined to conquer those they attacked.

Left: The smith and the weapons he wrought play an important part in the story of Sigurd Fafnisbane. Here the woodcarver has depicted Sigurd testing the sword with which he is going to kill the dragon. From the porch of Hylestad stave church, Norway, c. AD 1200.

Top: Axes with an inlay of silver were a status symbol for the most prominent Vikings. Mammen, Denmark.

Right: During the latter half of the ninth century, Norway became one united realm - this unification was achieved with the aid of sword and battle, and exactly the same means were employed when Christianity was introduced a couple of centuries later. To quote the law of the day: "A man must possess a battle-axe or sword, as well as a spear and a shield ..."

Swords and Ships

Surely no worse calamity could befall the princes and people of western Europe than an attack by the Vikings. Their ships drew little water, and thus they could sail not only along the coasts of the North Sea, but also on rivers far inland - both Paris and London were raided.

They were pagans, and as such they showed no greater respect for churches and monasteries than for any other buildings. They were after gold, silver and other costly goods, and often the cross would indicate that precious items were to be found nearby.

The approach of Viking ships must have been viewed with great fear - but relief must have been *still greater* when the Vikings proved to come as peaceful merchants. *Trade* went hand in hand with *transport* of merchandise, transport on board ship. The Vikings were sea-farers and ship-builders, and their experience in these fields formed an essential background for their activities as merchant traders, and as founders of cities.

Top right: This figure of a Viking was carved on an Anglo-Saxon cross during the tenth century. With one hand he holds a woman by the neck - in the other he has his sword. His intentions can hardly have been the most peaceable! This stone is from the churchyard at Weston in North Yorkshire.

Left: "Sword in the Rock." The work of Fritz Røed, this monument stands at Hafrsfjord in Norway.

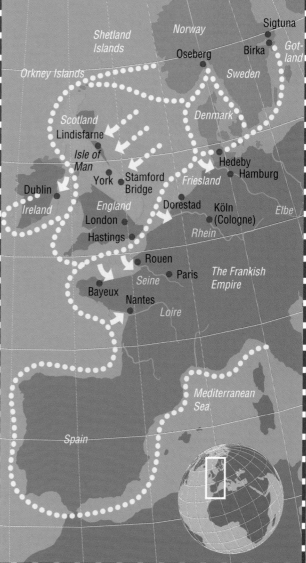

The Islands beyond the Skerries

The people of western Norway jocularly use this phrase of the British Isles. The first farmers to cross the North Sea towards the end of the eighth century may well have thought of Britain in this way. Sailing for no more than a couple of days would bring them to *Orkney* and *Shetland,* off the north coast of Scotland. Here they found a climate and a landscape very similar to those they were familiar with from home. By the end of the ninth century they had completely overpowered the original islanders, and had made their homes here. An *earl - jarl -* a member of a powerful family in Norway, ruled over the islands.

Now emigration from Norway spread to the *Hebrides, the Isle of Man* and parts of Scotland, Ireland and England. Thousands of Norse place-names, as well as men's and women's burials, testify to the Vikings' presence here.

The Isle of Man, in the Irish Sea, is very proud of its Viking roots, which we may see from their stamps. The necklace of glass beads was found in a Viking Age woman's grave.

Left: This stone from Lindisfarne is by way of being a sculptor's illustration of the earliest accounts of the Vikings' raids in England. In the Anglo-Saxon Chronicle we find the following entry for the year 793: "... the harrying of the heathen miserably destroyed God's church in Lindisfarne by rapine and slaughter."

The Viking kings of England struck their first coins at the end of the ninth century. The coin at the top was minted in Dublin by Sigtrygg Silkbeard in about 997; the next was struck in about 940 in York, by Aethelfred, Olaf Guthfrithsson's moneyer.

Kings and Realms

As time went by, the Vikings started to find burning and harrying less essential to their activities; they now offered their victims what one might well call a form of blackmail: *Pay, and we shall keep the peace!* English museums have very few Anglo-Saxon coins from this period - Scandinavian museums own an abundance!

In 991, a fleet of 93 Viking ships, led by the Norwegian chieftain *Olaf*, attacked Essex. When the English paid Olaf *five tons of silver*, they were left in peace - for a while. Three years later he returned, this time together with the King of Denmark, *Sven Forkbeard*. Now the price of peace had risen to eight tons of silver! Olaf sailed home with his fleet, and became King of Norway, adding the patronymic *Tryggvason* to his name. Sven continued to bring pressure to bear on the English, and in 1013 he conquered all England. He was succeeded by his son *Knut the Great*, known in England as King Canute - he became king of England, Denmark and Norway. No king in the North ever equalled him in power.

When King Edward died in 1066, without heirs, Harold Godwinson succeeded to the English throne. But when the news of this reached Harald the Hardruler, the King of Norway, he claimed the English crown. He sailed to England with a fleet of three hundred ships, and fought the English at Stamford Bridge, not far from York. In that battle Harald the Hardruler lost his life. From a painting by P.N.Arbo, 1870.

Top: Comb making was one of the crafts carried out by specialists in Dublin.

Below: Excavations in Dublin, Ireland. The city started as a fortified Viking camp, built when the Vikings spent the winter of 841 there. Dublin, like York, was to become the capital of a Norse kingdom.

The Realm of the Franks

In 810 Godfred, King of Denmark, sailed out with a fleet of *two hundred ships*. He sacked *Friesland*, part of the Frankish realm, levied taxes and received 50 kilograms of silver.

The Vikings had attacked the coasts of the Frankish empire - which extended as far north as the Danish frontier - many a time in the course of the ninth century, sacking Dorestad, Hamburg, Treves and Rouen. The coast of Normandy was particularly vulnerable. From this coast they sailed up the river Seine, staying there for the winter. They plundered Paris, and attacked La Cité, the city's fortification. But there they were stopped by Charles the Bald, who offered them *three tons of silver*. They sailed up the rivers, pillaging on the way. Following the river Loire they reached Nantes, the Rhine took them to Cologne.

France has yielded few archaeological finds representing the Vikings. But of course these raiders did not go to the realm of the Franks in order to *take* things there, nor in order to *leave anything behind* - their chief intent was that of *confiscating and removing valuables*. But they are represented by *place-names* - they gave new names to the places where they settled, in order to establish their right of ownership.

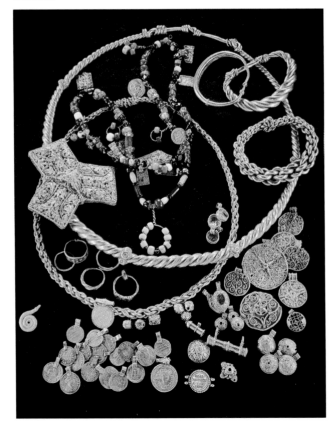

This gold treasure, which weighs 2.5 kg, consists very largely of "ransom" which the Vikings had extorted. It had been buried in the ground at Hon in Norway. The trefoil-shaped object is originally Frankish.

The Viking names of places and farms still exist today. Toutainville, for instance, comes from the Norse name Torstein, so that there can be no doubt that this was once his farm.

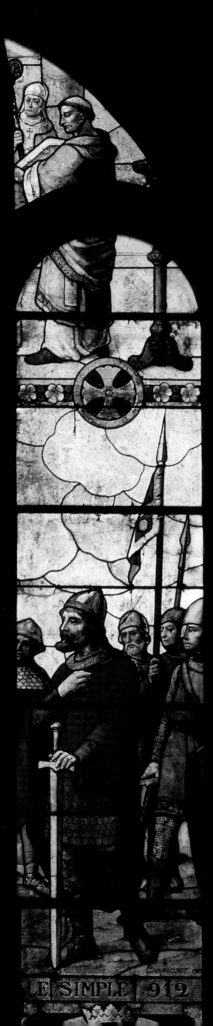

The Viking chieftain Rollo controlled the mouth of the river Seine. Charles the Simple, having exacted a vow of loyalty, bestowed on Rollo the title of Count of Rouen and gave him the surrounding lands. This brought the raids of the Vikings to an end, and was to lead to the establishment of the Duchy of Normandy. The early twentieth-century stained glass window from the church of St.Clair also shows the baptism of Rollo. Once baptised, he decided to be Frankish, and he changed his name to *Robert*.

TRAITE ENTRE · CHARLES · LE SIMPLE 912

MAGN O : NAVIGIO :

From Normandy against England

But the Vikings had an alternative: at times, they went into the service of foreign powers, rather than harrying on their own account. In other words, they served as mercenaries. Their pay might vary -

sometimes they were paid in precious metal, at others, they were given land to rule. It is easy to understand the abhorrence felt by the subjugated peoples, when we read, to quote the annals, that "heathen pirates, who had brought great misery upon the Christians, were appointed to lead Christian lands and the Church of Christ."

Adding up the figures cited in all the Frankish sources, we find that the Vikings were paid *310 kilograms* of gold, and *19 500* of silver!

William I was the son of Rollo's grandson's grandson. In 1066, he was Duke of Normandy, but by the end of that year, he had conquered England. His descendants have held the English throne

ever since. William the Conqueror, the Battle of Hastings and all the events connected with the conquest are illustrated in detail on an embroidered, 70 m long tapestry (*above*), which is on display in Bayeux in France today. Even though much blood beside that of the Vikings must have flown in the veins of William and his men after five generations or

MAR

more, the tapestry shows
that many Norse features
survived.

Birka

In a large area on *the island of Björkö in Lake Mälar* -part of a great waterway which runs from far inland in Central Sweden to the Baltic by Stockholm - great many ancient monuments and other archaeological finds

Hedeby-coins found at Birka.

have come to light. This is where the town of Birka, the most prominent of all the Scandinavian Viking Age market centres, lay. Its situation was ideal, close to the Baltic and the eastern trade routes, as well as to those leading south, to Hedeby and the Continent. The situation of this fortified town afforded protection from the coast. More than a thousand people, all of them artisans and merchants, lived here. Birka had piers where ships could lay to, and a fortified outcrop above the town provided a good means of defence. Excavations on the island, of varying extent, have been going on ever since the 1680s, the most recent during the first half of the 1990s.

Ansgar, a Frankish monk, visited the town twice as a missionary, in 830 and in 851. It is from the accounts about him that we know the name *Birka*. He founded a Christian congregation here and raised a chapel, but the results of his efforts were not to last. Even so, Ansgar was the first to be known as the Apostle of the North.

When designing the Birka stamps in 1990, the sources employed by the artist Svenolov Ehrén included motifs from carved stones from Gotland.

SVERIGE

SVERIGE

2.50

SO EHREN

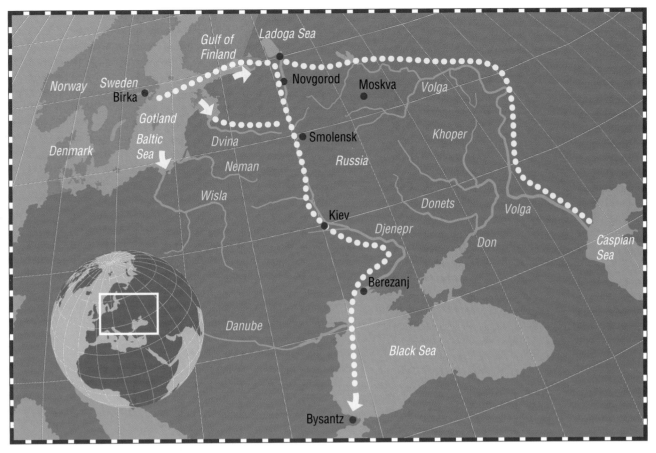

The Route to the East

Two rune-stones stand by the road in Täby, north of Stockholm. They were raised by Östen's widow and their three sons. The inscriptions tell us that he "journeyed to Jerusalem, and died in Greece". The cross bears out the worthy intent of his voyage - he was on a pilgrimage to the Holy Land.

The inscription takes us back to the beginning of the eleventh century, the century when the majority of Sweden's rune-stones - more than three thousand in all - were raised. As many of them commemorate close relatives who died in foreign lands, they also serve as monuments to the daring voyages to Russia, the Caspian Sea, the Black Sea and the Mediterranean.

The great rivers running east had become the normal trade routes between the Orient and western Europe long before the advent of the Viking Age, but it was not until the eleventh century that the Vikings started to take such an active part in this trade.

Left: Sweden - and especially Gotland - has yielded a great number of buried silver hoards of oriental origin. 70 000 Arabic coins, and 6 000 Byzantine ones, have been found in Sweden.

to ten metres long, no larger than that they could be hauled through the rapids. Or over *isthmuses* for that matter, for in some places one had to cross necks of land before one could sail on on the Dnieper or the Volga. It was a great advantage if the merchandise included slaves, for they could make themselves useful as oarsmen, or during a passage over land. The cargo also included furs, honey, wax and weapons. Payment was in the form of silver - this the Vikings weighed on balances (**left**). Such balances have been found in Viking women's graves in Russia, which would suggest that women also took part in this trade.

By Boat - over Water and Land

The lands by the vast rivers to the east were most easily reached by way of the Gulf of Finland. With ships as large as those on which the Vikings crossed the North Sea, they could sail as far as to *Staraja Ladoga*. But there they had to stop, and transfer to smaller boats. Nor were they allowed to pass without paying. Prince *Oleg*, who ruled in Russia from 882 until 912, controlled all traffic from a castle by the river-bank. He was of Scandinavian descent, and his Norse name was *Helge*. Ten per cent of the population of Staraja Ladoga were *Rus*, the name by which the Scandinavians were known, and from which the name *Russia* derives.

Some of the Viking barrows in *Smolensk* are raised over boats up

The Vikings in Trade and in Politics

The Scandinavian graves in Russia were the last resting places of Vikings who never returned to their homes. At home, their widows, fathers and children erected rune-stones in their memory. But many of the Norse burials in Russia are women's graves, which would seem to show that entire families voyaged east. A fact worth remembering in this context is that at first, Russia had been organised and led by Swedish Vikings.

Below: This runic inscription from the island of Berezanj, where the Dnieper runs out into the Black Sea, commemorates a Viking buried there: "Grane made this stone coffin for Karl, his friend."

Far right: The Vikings called Byzantium by the respectful name of Miklagard - the big city. The Emperor's life-guards included a company of Vikings. Perhaps the Halfdan who scratched his name on the edge of a marble slab in Hagia Sofia was a member of this company?

Right: Another Viking left a runic message at Pireus, the harbour of Athens, but this inscription cannot be deciphered.

Right: After St.Olaf, the King of Norway, had fallen in the battle of Stiklestad in 1030, his half-brother Harald fled to Byzantium (Istanbul), where he served in the Emperor's guards. Fifteen years later he returned to Norway and claimed the throne, as King Harald the Hardruler. His queen was Ellisiv, whose father was Jaroslav, Grand Duke of Kiev.

The "Viking"

Inspired by the Gokstad Ship, which had been excavated in 1880, Captain Magnus Andersen had a replica built, the "Viking". In 1893 he sailed from Norway with a crew of eleven, in order to show that the Vinland voyages of which the sagas tell could well have been accomplished with ships of this type. Four weeks after they had left Norway, the "Viking" berthed in Chicago. Her seaworthiness had been proved beyond doubt, her average speed was five to six knots, but she could make as much as eleven knots.

Since then, about thirty replicas of Viking ships have been built. They have shown us more than what the sagas can tell.

*Ragnar Thorseth from Norway (**right**) has had three replicas made. With one of these, "Saga Siglar", he circumnavigated the world. (See also pages 22 and 25).*

K. Bergslien – Christiania 1869

On Skis

Once snow covers the land, *skis* make rapid travel easy. Without skis, there is no point in even trying to travel on foot in winter. Skis even had a god of their own - this shows how important they were. *Ull* was the god of skis - he was Thor's stepson, and he surpassed all others in skiing and in the use of bow and arrow.

This Viking Age ski was found at Badstusund in Sweden. Skis occur in a number of other archaeological finds, showing that skiing had ancient traditions in the North.

Knud Bergslien painted "The Birchlegs on Skis, taking the infant Håkon Håkonsøn to Trondhjem" in 1869. Although the motif does not refer to the Viking Age, the dramatic political situation, which affected all of Norway during the thirteenth century, illustrates the enormous importance of skis.